YOUR UNIQUE DESIGN

CLASS GUIDE

SHIRLEY GILES DAVIS

Design by Ashley Anna Matthews.

ISBN: 978-0-578-59019-6

All Scriptures referenced are from the New International Version of the Bible, 2011, by Zondervan, unless otherwise noted.

Table of Contents

Introduction

This course is designed to help you learn more about how God sees you, to discover your spiritual gifts, and to explore living and serving that reflects your unique design.

God loves you. He has been intentional in creating you. His desire is that you flourish in every sphere in which you find yourself.

In the Lord's power and gifting, you are made able to do that which you are designed to do. God calls. God equips. We respond.

Together with others in your faith community, this two-session course can be transformative—for you and for your church as you discover how God wants you to engage with His purposes in your life, your church, and this world!

How to Use These Materials

This guidebook accompanies the Your Unique Design classes. The course covers the Biblical foundations undergirding how God has uniquely created, called, and equipped each of His followers. The material also aids each person in discovering his/her God-given spiritual gifts as well as giving practical ways to live into each person's individual calling and purpose.

Each participant in a Your Unique Design class needs their own Your Unique Design Class Guide. Each session takes 1-1.5 hours, including discussion times.

For Leaders: You will also need a copy of the Your Unique Design Facilitator Guide containing class scripts and more information about designing and implementing the Your Unique Design course at your church.

Session One
Introducing Gifts

Group Exercise

WRITE DOWN ONE THING YOU HOPE TO GET OUT OF THESE TWO SESSIONS ABOUT YOUR OWN UNIQUE DESIGN:

Biblical Foundations

YOU ARE UNIQUE: CREATED UNIQUELY AND SPECIALLY BY GOD

PSALM 139:13-18 | For you created my inmost being; you knit me together in my mother's womb. I praise you because I am fearfully and wonderfully made; your works are wonderful, I know that full well. My frame was not hidden from you when I was made in the secret place. When I was woven together in the depths of the earth, your eyes saw my unformed body. All the days ordained for me were written in your book before one of them came to be.

YOU ARE LOVED

EPHESIANS 3:17-19 | Paul prays that we "may have power... to grasp how wide and long and high and deep is the love of Christ, and to know this love that surpasses knowledge..."

EPHESIANS 5:1 | Calls us "dearly loved children."

YOU ARE CALLED...CHOSEN...SET APART

1 CORINTHIANS 6:11 | Now your sins have been washed away...you have been set apart for God.

EPHESIANS 2:10 | For we are God's handiwork, created in Christ Jesus to do good works, which God prepared in advance for us to do.

HE CALLS...AND...HE EQUIPS

HEBREWS 13:20-21| Now may the God of peace, who through the blood of the eternal covenant brought back from the dead our Lord Jesus, that great Shepherd of the sheep, equip you with everything good for doing his will, and may he work in us what is pleasing to him, through Jesus Christ, to whom be glory for ever and ever. Amen.

SPIRITUAL GIFTS

Greek Terminology:

The primary scriptural basis for spiritual gifts is found in:

Romans 12
1 Corinthians 12-14
Ephesians 4
1 Peter 4

Spiritual Gifts are (from those passages):
- Special abilities; spiritual, beyond our natural talents.
- Given/distributed by God according to His choosing, His grace, His mercy.
- Through the Holy Spirit — Spirit empowered.
- To each and every believer in Jesus.
- In order to be used to glorify God.
- For the common good and strengthening of the Body of Christ.
- Given to you for others; you benefit but it's not about you.

1 CORINTHIANS 12:1 | Now about the gifts of the Spirit, brothers and sisters, I do not want you to be uninformed...

1 CORINTHIANS 12:4-11 | There are different kinds of gifts, but the same Spirit distributes them. There are different kinds of service, but the same Lord. There are different kinds of working, but in all of them and in everyone it is the same God at work. Now to each one the manifestation of the Spirit is given for the common good. To one there is given through the Spirit a message of wisdom, to another a message of knowledge by means of the same Spirit, to another faith by the same Spirit, to another gifts of healing by that one Spirit, to another miraculous powers, to another prophecy, to another distinguishing between spirits, to another speaking in different kinds of tongues [languages] and to still another the interpretation of tongues [languages]. All these are the work of one and the same Spirit, and he distributes them to each one, just as he determines.

CALLED TO SERVE CHRIST WITH THE WHOLE OF OURSELVES

ROMANS 12:1-2 | Therefore, I urge you, brothers and sisters, in view of God's mercy, to offer your bodies as a living sacrifice, holy and pleasing to God—this is your true and proper worship. Do not conform to the pattern of this world, but be transformed by the renewing of your mind. Then you will be able to test and approve what God's will is—his good, pleasing and perfect will.

COLOSSIANS 3:23-24 | Whatever you do, work at it with all of your heart, as working for the Lord, not for human masters, since you know that you will receive an inheritance from the Lord as a reward. It is the Lord Christ you are serving.

Spiritual Gifts Assessment

Go to **GODGIFTSYOU.COM** and click on Assessment. Once you complete all of the questions, you will receive a results page as well as an email containing those same scores. Take a moment to record your highest and lowest scoring gifts below.

Your Spiritual Gifts Assessment Results

SPIRITUAL GIFTS	TOP 3-5 (A-W)	LOW 2 (A-S)	GIFTS AFFIRMED BY OTHERS
A | ADMINISTRATION			
B | APOSTLESHIP			
C | ARTISTIC EXPRESSION			
D | CRAFTSMANSHIP			
E | DISCERNMENT			
F | EVANGELISM			
G | EXHORTATION			
H | FAITH			
I | GIVING			
J | HELPS			
K | HOSPITALITY			
L | INTERCESSION			
M | KNOWLEDGE			
N | LEADERSHIP			
O | MERCY			
P | PROPHECY			
Q | SHEPHERDING			
R | TEACHING			
S | WISDOM			
T | HEALING			
U | MIRACULOUS POWERS			
V | TONGUES			
W | INTERPRETATION OF TONGUES			

(Alternative: Take the same gifts assessment and score it yourself. See Appendix A on page 33.)

Spiritual Gifts Overview

Gift	Brief Definition Those with gifts of...	Description	Someone with Gift:
Administration	...bring efficiency and order to the church and to other organizations. These are usually the planners, goal-setters, or managers. They look for new ways to help people and tasks be more effective.	Organizer Strategizer Developer	
Apostleship	...introduce new ministries to the church. They blaze new trails, pioneer new endeavors, and step out into uncharted territory. They may have a great desire to reach out to unreached peoples and to spread the vision of the mission of the church.	Starter Entrepreneur Pioneer	
Artistic Expression	...have a special ability to communicate God's message through the fine arts, including drama, creative writing, music, and drawing. Through their God-given creativity, they use their gifts to draw others in and focus on God, His creation, and His message.	Expressive Innovative Creative	
Craftsmanship	...are uniquely skilled at working with raw materials, helping to create things that are used for ministry or that help meet tangible needs. They can be found fixing, remodeling, and sprucing up buildings, and/or creating and stitching items—honoring God and benefitting His people in practical ways.	Skilled Creative Resourceful	
Discernment	...distinguish between good and evil, truth and error, right and wrong. These people provide much-needed insight, point out inconsistencies in the teaching of God's Word, challenge deceitfulness in others, help sort out impure motives from pure ones, and identify spiritual warfare.	Intuitive Perceptive Sensitive	

Gift	Brief Definition Those with gifts of...	Description	Someone with Gift:
Evangelism	...seem to be always seeking to build meaningful relationships with non-believers and are often able to steer conversations with these people to spiritual things. They communicate the good news of Jesus to unbelievers in such a way that they see people believe and commit to following Christ.	Forthright Influential Heart for the lost	
Exhortation	...offer a word of hope combined with a gentle push to action to those who are discouraged, tentative, or needing direction. People with this gift come alongside to offer reassurance and affirmation, and, when needed, to challenge or confront, all with the goal of seeing others grow to greater maturity in their faith.	Affirming Motivator Heartening	
Faith	...have that extra measure of confidence in God and His promises, helping inspire others to greater belief. Those with this gift live constantly in the knowledge that God works all things for their good and the good of others who are called according to His purposes.	Believing Hopeful Secure	
Giving	...have an extra measure of the ability to be generous. People with this gift live as if everything they have belongs to God, knowing that God will provide for their needs. Giving may involve money as well as other resources like housing, food, clothing, etc.	Resourceful Sacrificial Steward	
Helps	...meet the practical needs of others and of the church/organizations in order to enhance, support, or accomplish ministry. Indicators of someone with the gift of helps are that he/she serves willingly, cheerfully, humbly, and wherever needed.	Humble Available Dependable	

Gift	Brief Definition Those with gifts of...	Description	Someone with Gift:
Hospitality	...have the divine ability to make people feel welcome and accepted--anywhere at any time. People with this gift enjoy connecting people with each other and creating an atmosphere where relationships and community can flourish.	Accepting Welcoming Friendly	
Intercession	...feel compelled by God to pray on a daily basis for others. They are completely convinced of the awesome power and necessity of prayer. They pray as a first response to any given situation, during that situation, and afterwards.	Faithful Trusting Aware	
Knowledge	...bring Biblical truth and God-given insight to the church. They may also receive a word from God that is uniquely timed and tailored for a given situation. People with the gift of knowledge may also be those who have a keen desire to study and know God's Word, and God may use this understanding of Scripture to speak a word of knowledge to a person or group.	Aware Perceptive Student of Scripture	
Leadership	...are visionary, good motivators, and effective directors—helping inspire others to achieve God's purpose. Leadership involves not only having a vision of the preferred future for the church or an organization, but also having clarity on next steps to achieve that vision, the ability to communicate vision in a way that inspires others, and equip the rest of the team to pursue the same direction together.	Visionary Goal-oriented Credible	
Mercy	...provide comfort, support, and presence to those who are suffering, in crisis, or otherwise hurting. Those with this gift reach out to others who are broken. They show God's heart to those who need the empathy of a listening ear.	Caring Compassionate Kind	

Gift	Brief Definition Those with gifts of...	Description	Someone with Gift:
Prophecy	...have the gift that God uses to convict His people of sin and their need for repentance. Prophecy brings warning, challenge, correction, and confrontation without compromise.	Exposes Challenges Bold	
Shepherding	...provide nurture and guidance to others so that they grow in spiritual maturity and Christ-like character. People with the shepherding gift seek to walk alongside someone for a long or short season and direct them to Jesus and His offer of life, hope, and peace.	Fosters health Guide Counselor	
Teaching	...study, understand, explain, and apply Scripture's truths in such a way that people grow in their own understanding, are challenged, and are inspired to apply what they've learned. This can be done in a church or other context, since God's truth is true everywhere.	Communi-cator Inspiring Applies learning	
Wisdom	...use their God-given insight and information by applying it to specific situations, providing guidance in the church. They see the right course of action in the midst of otherwise confusing or overwhelming circumstances. Input from those with wisdom can shift a group's direction or help guide someone toward greater clarity.	Guide Perceptive Good judg-ment	
Healing	...follow the pattern we see in the life and ministry of Jesus where healing was physical, mental, emotional, and/or spiritual. Often also used by God to authenticate a message or a ministry. Always it is to show God's grace and mercy and power.	Restorer Responsive Intercessor	

Gift	Brief Definition Those with gifts of...	Description	Someone with Gift:
Miraculous Powers	...help authenticate a ministry, encourage a body of believers, and show the power of God. In the life and ministry of Jesus, His miracles included feeding the multitudes, turning water into wine, raising the dead and walking on water.	Responsive Courageous Alert	
Tongues	...may speak in other languages as the Spirit enables them (Acts 2); may speak in an unknown language (that of "angels"- 1 Cor. 13); may speak to God in tongues (1 Cor. 13). It can also be a way of "uttering the mysteries of the Spirit," and "sounding a clear call" to God's people (1 Cor. 14). Usually accompanied by the Interpretation of Tongues gift.	Responsive Expressive Worshipful	
Interpretation of Tongues	...help the rest of the Body of Christ understand the message being spoken by those with the gift of Tongues. May be given concurrently to someone with Tongues.	Responsive Obedient Discerning	

Group Exercise

REPORTING ON SPIRITUAL GIFTS DISCOVERED

SHARE YOUR TOP RESULTS

WHAT WERE CONFIRMATIONS OF WHAT YOU ALREADY KNEW?

WHAT WERE SURPRISES? (WHAT SHOWED UP ON YOUR LIST THAT YOU DIDN'T EXPECT? WHAT DIDN'T SHOW UP THAT YOU THOUGHT WAS AN AREA OF GIFTEDNESS?)

ANY DISAPPOINTMENTS? (ARE YOU DISAPPOINTED WITH YOUR LIST OF GIFTS IN SOME WAY?)

SHARE YOUR LOWEST SCORING ONE(S) - WHAT WAS NOT A GIFT FOR YOU?

JOT DOWN ONE OR TWO THINGS YOU WANT TO REMEMBER FROM THIS SESSION-ABOUT YOUR UNIQUENESS, GOD'S CALL, YOUR BEING SET APART, BEING EQUIPPED, ABOUT THE BODY OF CHRIST...WHATEVER GOD BRINGS TO MIND.

READ 1 CORINTHIANS 12.

Homework

Complete the FINDING GIFTS exercise below. (Est. time: 10-15 minutes.)

1. FOR THE FOLLOWING THREE PASSAGES, CIRCLE THE ACTIVITIES YOU NOTE AND JOT DOWN A POSSIBLE THEME THAT YOU SEE IN ALL THREE:

Praise him with the sounding of the trumpet, praise him with the harp and lyre, praise him with timbrel and dancing, praise him with strings and pipe, praise him with the clash of cymbals, praise him with resounding cymbals (Psalm 150:3-5).

Then Miriam the prophet, Aaron's sister, took a timbrel in her hand, and all the women followed her, with timbrels and dancing. Miriam sang to them: "Sing to the Lord, for he is highly exalted. Both horse and driver he has hurled into the sea" (Exodus 15:20-21).

Wearing a linen ephod, David was dancing before the Lord with all his might, while he and Israel were bringing up the ark of the Lord with shouts and the sound of trumpets (2 Samuel 6:14-15).

2. FOR THE FOLLOWING THREE PASSAGES, WHAT IS THE GIFT MENTIONED OR IMPLIED?

Epaphras, who is one of you and a servant of Christ Jesus, sends greetings. He is always wrestling in prayer for you, that you may stand firm in all the will of God, mature and fully assured (Colossians 4:12).

I have not stopped giving thanks for you, remembering you in my prayers (Ephesians 1:16).

I thank God, whom I serve, as my ancestors did, with a clear conscience, as night and day, I constantly remember you in my prayers (2 Timothy 1:3).

3. CIRCLE THE SPIRTUAL GIFTS MENTIONED OR IMPLIED IN EACH OF THE FOLLOWING PASSAGES.

Now the Lord spoke to Moses, saying, "See, I have called by name Bezalel, the son of Uri, the son of Hur, of the tribe of Judah. I have filled him with the Spirit of God in wisdom, in understanding, in knowledge, and in all kinds of craftsmanship, to make artistic designs for work in gold, in silver, and in bronze, and in the cutting of stones for settings, and in the carving of wood, that he may work in all kinds of craftsmanship (Exodus 31:1-5, NASB).

Now to each one the manifestation of the Spirit is given for the common good. To one there is given through the Spirit a message of wisdom, to another a message of knowledge by means of the same Spirit, to another faith by the same Spirit, to another gifts of healing by that one Spirit, to another miraculous powers, to another prophecy, to another distinguishing between spirits, to another speaking in different kinds of tongues and to still another the interpretation of tongues. All these are the work of one and the same Spirit, and he distributes them to each one, just as he determines (1 Corinthians 12:7-11).

Now you are the body of Christ, and each one of you is a part of it. And God has placed in the church first of all apostles, second prophets, third teachers, then miracles, then gifts of healing, of helping, of guidance, and of different kinds of tongues. Are all apostles? Are all prophets? Are all teachers? Do all work miracles? Do all have gifts of healing? Do all speak in tongues? Do all interpret? (1 Corinthians 12:27-30.)

Offer hospitality to one another without grumbling. Each of you should use whatever gift you have received to serve others, as faithful stewards of God's grace in its various forms. If anyone speaks, they should do so as one who speaks the very words of God. If anyone serves, they should do so with the strength God provides, so that in all things God may be praised through Jesus Christ. To him be the glory and the power for ever and ever. Amen (1 Peter 4:9-11).

For just as each of us has one body with many members, and these members do not all have the same function, so in Christ we, though many, form one body, and each member belongs to all the others. We have different gifts, according to the grace given to each of us. If your gift is prophesying, then prophesy in accordance with your faith; if it is serving, then serve; if it is teaching, then teach; if it is to encourage, then give encouragement; if it is giving, then give generously; if it is to lead, do it diligently; if it is to show mercy, do it cheerfully (Romans 12:4-8).

Some of us have been given special ability as apostles; to others he has given the gift of being able to preach well; some have special ability in winning people to Christ, helping them to trust him as their Savior; still others have a gift for caring for God's people as a shepherd does his sheep, leading and teaching them in the ways of God. Why is it that he gives us these special abilities to do certain things best? It is that God's people will be equipped to do better work for him, building up the Church, the body of Christ, to a position of strength and maturity; until finally we all believe alike about our salvation and about our Savior, God's Son, and all become full-grown in the Lord—yes, to the point of being filled full with Christ (Ephesians 4:11-13; NLT).

FOR FURTHER STUDY (OPTIONAL)

Read...

1 Corinthians 12-14
Romans 12
Ephesians 4
1 Peter 4

Gifts-Calling-Purpose blog: https://godgiftsyou.com/blog/

Study

Work through a copy of the six-week study guide/workbook: God. Gifts. You. Your Unique Calling and Design (available on Amazon and through   God-GiftsYou.com).

Each week is designed with five days of homework. Six video teaching sessions are available to accompany the study, and a Small Group Discussion Guide is provided weekly. This study is intended both as a workbook and an ongoing resource for those seeking to go deeper in understanding and living out the Biblical mandate of being the Body of Christ.

Session 2
Recognizing and Affirming Gifts

Body of Christ

CONTEXT OF THE CHURCH AS THE BODY OF CHRIST

1 CORINTHIANS 12:12-30 | Just as a body, though one, has many parts, but all its many parts form one body so it is with Christ. For we were all baptized by one Spirit so as to form one body—whether Jews or Gentiles, slave or free—and we were all given the one Spirit to drink. Even so the body is not made up of one part but of many.

Now if the foot should say, "Because I am not a hand, I do not belong to the body," it would not for that reason stop being part of the body. And if the ear should say, "Because I am not an eye, I do not belong to the body," it would not for that reason stop being part of the body. If the whole body were an eye, where would the sense of hearing be? If the whole body were an ear, where would the sense of smell be? But in fact God has placed the parts in the body, every one of them, just as he wanted them to be. If they were all one part, where would the body be? As it is, there are many parts, but one body.

The eye cannot say to the hand, "I don't need you!" And the head cannot say to the feet, "I don't need you!" On the contrary, those parts of the body that seem to be weaker are indispensable, and the parts that we think are less honorable we treat with special honor. And the parts that are unpresentable are treated with special modesty, while our presentable parts need no special treatment. But God has put the body together, giving greater honor to the parts that lacked it, so that there should be no division in the body, but that its parts should have equal concern for each other. If one part suffers, every part suffers with it; if one part is honored, every part rejoices with it.

Now you are the body of Christ, and each one of you is a part of it. And God has placed in the church first of all apostles, second prophets, third teachers, then miracles, then gifts of healing, of helping, of guidance, and of different kinds of tongues. Are all apostles? Are all prophets? Are all teachers? Do all work miracles? Do all have gifts of healing? Do all speak in tongues? Do all interpret?

WAYS IN WHICH THE BODY ANALOGY APPLIES TO THE CHURCH:

Group Exercise

BODY PARTS ACTIVITY—WHAT PART OF THE BODY ARE YOU?

TAKE A MOMENT OF SILENCE TO REFLECT ON WHAT YOU BRING TO THIS BODY OF CHRIST. THINK IN TERMS OF THE PARTS OF THE HUMAN BODY AND THEIR FUNCTIONS. THE GRAPHIC BELOW MAY BE USEFUL.

LEG | FOOT	EYE	EAR
GUT | STOMACH	HEART	BRAIN
MOUTH	ARM | HAND	OTHER

SHARE YOUR CHOICE WITH OTHERS AT YOUR TABLE.

INTERDEPENDENCE

Diversity | Unity:

Group Exercise

LOVE

AT YOUR TABLES, READ TOGETHER 1 CORINTHIANS 13:1-8. DISCUSS WHAT STANDS OUT TO YOU, KEEPING IN MIND THE CONTEXT WAS UNDERSTANDING AND LIVING INTO USE OF SPIRITUAL GIFTS.

1 CORINTHIANS 13:1-8 | IF I SPEAK IN THE TONGUES OF MEN OR OF ANGELS, BUT DO NOT HAVE LOVE, I AM ONLY A RESOUNDING GONG OR A CLANGING CYMBAL. IF I HAVE THE GIFT OF PROPHECY AND CAN FATHOM ALL MYSTERIES AND ALL KNOWLEDGE, AND IF I HAVE A FAITH THAT CAN MOVE MOUNTAINS, BUT DO NOT HAVE LOVE, I AM NOTHING. IF I GIVE ALL I POSSESS TO THE POOR AND GIVE OVER MY BODY TO HARDSHIP THAT I MAY BOAST, BUT DO NOT HAVE LOVE, I GAIN NOTHING.

LOVE IS PATIENT, LOVE IS KIND. IT DOES NOT ENVY, IT DOES NOT BOAST, IT IS NOT PROUD. IT DOES NOT DISHONOR OTHERS, IT IS NOT SELF-SEEKING, IT IS NOT EASILY ANGERED, IT KEEPS NO RECORD OF WRONGS. LOVE DOES NOT DELIGHT IN EVIL BUT REJOICES WITH THE TRUTH. IT ALWAYS PROTECTS, ALWAYS TRUSTS, ALWAYS HOPES, ALWAYS PERSEVERES.

LOVE NEVER FAILS.

---

23 GIFTS

| Don't neglect.

| Stewards.

| Clarity.

| Meaning and connection.

| Church health.

DEBRIEFING GIFTS

Character of Christ...fruit of the spirit...spiritual disciplines vs. gifting.

Knowing your gifts can focus your "yes" or "no."

Assessment vs. aspects of gifts vs. confusion between roles and gifts.

Gifts are not natural talents:

| Common grace.

| Offer all of yourself.

YOUR TOP 3-5 GIFTS

| Get feedback.

| Awareness.

DEBRIEFING GIFTS

EXERCISE:

| TAKE **TWO MINUTES** TO SELECT OR CREATE AN ITEM THAT SYMBOLIZES WHAT YOU REALLY LOVE DOING, OR SOMETHING YOU BELIEVE YOU DO WELL.

| AFTER TWO MINUTES, **SHARE YOUR DISCOVERY** WITH THE OTHERS AT YOUR TABLE.

WHAT STIRS YOU? WHAT MOTIVATES YOU TO MAKE A COMMITTMENT?

TAKE A MOMENT TO JOT DOWN YOUR RESPONSE TO THIS QUESTION: WHAT HINTS ABOUT YOUR INTERESTS OR CALL DID THIS BRIEF EXERCISE UNEARTH OR REAFFIRM FOR YOU?

Gifts, Interests, Talents, Experience:
A Lifetime of Serving

IT ALL COUNTS

Gifts are the equipment God gives you to use to accomplish His purposes.

Call and motivation help you determine where and with whom you will serve.

Your unique behavioral style helps shape what your service looks like.

Talent(s) and life experience(s) add richness and direction.

APPLICATION

Affirmation.

New understanding/clarity and seeking a new place to serve.

Permission to focus efforts.

Confusion or need for more learning/discipleship.

Group Exercise

HELPING EACH OTHER IDENTIFY POSSIBLE AREAS OF MINISTRY

TABLE DISCUSSION GUIDE:

| HELP EACH OTHER DISCERN GIFTS AND CALL AND INTERESTS.

| SPEND TIME HELPING EACH OTHER BRAINSTORM IDEAS FOR SERVING OR FOCUSING MINISTRY. IT MIGHT BE HELPFUL TO THINK ABOUT: IF YOU ARE SERVING, WHAT DO YOU LOVE ABOUT IT? OR IF YOU ARE SEEKING TO SERVE, WHAT ARE YOU LOOKING FOR IN A SERVING OPPORTUNITY...AND WHERE DO YOUR GIFTS FIT?

JOT DOWN IDEAS FOR YOUR OWN SERVICE/ENGAGEMENT BELOW:

WHAT IS ONE STEP YOU CAN TAKE NOW?

OTHER RESOURCES

| Prayer.
| Bible.
| Your class leader.
| Your church website.
| Local nonprofit agencies and human services organizations.
| Keep an eye on your church bulletin/newsletter/weekly posts and worship announcements.
| Meet with a Gifts Coach.
| Do the six-week *God. Gifts. You. Your Unique Calling and Design* study with your small group. Available at **GODGIFTSYOU.COM**

ADDITIONAL GUIDANCE

| Try something!
| Recognize that it's a process.
| Don't give up.
| Your first response.
| Visible to others.
| Don't let guilt be a motivator.

1 PETER 4:10 | Each of you should use whatever gift you have received to serve others, as faithful stewards of God's grace in its various forms.

| Stewards of grace.

| In God's strength.

JOT DOWN what you want to remember from this session, or answer: In what ways are you feeling challenged about the discovery or use of your ministry gift(s)?

APPENDIX A

Spiritual Gifts Assessment

Please read each statement carefully and give each one a score (from 0 to 5) relative to how well the statement reflects your behavior/experience. Answer how you ARE not how you want to be. Transfer the numbers to the boxes on the Spiritual Gift Assessment Scoring Sheet, page 37.

0	1	2	3	4	5
Never true of me					True of me

1. _____ I am good at taking care of details that other people might neglect.

2. _____ I have been successful in starting new ministries.

3. _____ God uses my artistic/musical gifts to help people worship him.

4. _____ I enjoy working with my hands to create things that facilitate my own or another's ministry.

5. _____ When I hear somebody claim to be teaching from the Bible, I can usually tell whether the teaching is sound or unsound.

6. _____ When I talk to non-Christians about Jesus, they are often interested in what I have to say.

7. _____ I am able to motivate others to persevere in the face of discouragement and struggles.

8. _____ I am more confident than most that God will keep his promises.

9. _____ I rearrange things in my life in order to be able to give my financial or other resources more generously to God's work.

10. _____ When there is a job to be done, I am one of the first to jump in and volunteer.

11. _____ In gatherings of people, I tend to notice those at the margins and make them feel like they belong.

12. _____ People who know me consider me a "prayer warrior."

13. _____ Others look to me for my knowledge of Biblical concepts and/or my insight into situations.

14. _____ When the path forward for a group is uncertain, people look to me for leadership.

15. _____ Comforting those who are suffering comes naturally to me.

16. _____ I often say things that people in the church need to hear, even though it may make them uncomfortable.

17. _____ I have been able to successfully guide others in their spiritual journeys.

18. _____ I can explain Biblical truth to people in a way that allows them to "get it."

19. _____ People look to me for counsel when there are decisions to be made.

20. _____ When I see people who are sick, I have a strong desire to pray for their healing.

21. _____ I have seen God do something miraculous in connection with a prayer I have prayed.

22. _____ When I pray, sometimes words come out that I do not understand.

23. _____ When someone speaks in Tongues, I am able to understand the message.

24. _____ Others look to me for my organizational skills.

25. _____ When I see a need in the church or community, I envision how to create a ministry to meet the need.

26. _____ I can communicate important things about God to others through creative writing, art, or music.

27. _____ I am skilled at creating useful items from tangible materials like glass, metal, wood, paper, etc.

28. _____ I can tell when there is spiritual evil in a situation.

29. _____ Sharing the Gospel comes easily to me.

30. _____ People think of me as an encouraging friend.

31. _____ In the face of doubt or uncertainty, I persevere in doing the things God has called me to do.

32. _____ I frequently look for opportunities to contribute money or resources in a way that makes a difference.

33. _____ I do not particularly care what I'm doing to serve, as long as it helps further God's work in the church or the world.

34. _____ Either in my home or elsewhere, I create a welcoming atmosphere for others.

35. _____ When I learn about somebody in a difficult situation, my first impulse is to pray.

36. _____ I see the shades of gray in situations where others see black and white.

37. _____ I motivate others to come along with me as I pursue God's vision.

38. _____ My automatic response when someone is hurting is to come alongside and offer a listening ear and a shoulder to cry on.

39. _____ God sometimes leads me to ask difficult questions and point out inconvenient truths.

40. _____ I enjoy coming alongside someone in one-on-one mentoring.

41. _____ I am able to connect God's truth with today's life situations.

42. _____ I can usually see the wise course of action to take.

43. _____ I have seen God heal someone in connection with a prayer I have prayed or by my laying on of hands.

44. _____ I have sometimes felt powerfully led by God to perform an extraordinary act.

45. _____ Praying privately in Tongues builds my personal faith and helps me feel closer to God.

46. _____ I am able to provide the meaning of a message of Tongues to others present.

47. _____ If somebody has a good vision, I can do the work of putting it into practice.

48. _____ I have been told I exhibit an entrepreneurial capacity.

49. _____ I express something of God's creativity through dance, imaginative writing, painting, drawing, or drama.

50. _____ Others depend on me to make or fix things.

51. _____ Others have told me that I have a strong intuitive sense, seeing dangers or opportunities that others miss.

52. _____ I actively develop relationships with and reach out to those outside the church community.

53. _____ I enjoy helping people take steps toward greater maturity in any aspect of their lives.

54. _____ In situations where others might doubt God, I do not.

55. _____ Although my generosity is usually meant to be anonymous, people know me as charitable and philanthropic with the resources God has given me.

56. _____ I enjoy doing the behind-the-scenes things that support others' ministries.

57. _____ Others have noticed that I am good at making people feel welcome and accepted wherever I go.

58. _____ I am one of the first people others turn to when asking for prayer.

59. _____ I often see important aspects of Biblical passages that others do not recognize.

60. _____ I inspire others to pursue goals that I clearly articulate.

61. _____ People describe me as compassionate and empathic.

62. _____ God uses me to point out his plans and purposes when others may be straying from the path.

63. _____ I find satisfaction in long-term coaching relationships.

64. _____ Others have consistently said that they have learned from or been challenged by my teaching.

65. _____ I am rarely confused about what next steps to take in challenging situations.

66. _____ I am drawn to participate in ministries like "inner healing prayer" or "spiritual deliverance healing."

67. _____ God has authenticated a message or ministry by working through me to perform something supernatural.

68. _____ I have spoken about faith in a language that is not my native tongue, and felt like God was enabling my fluency.

69. _____ If someone prays in Tongues, I get a feeling or vision or picture of what the message means.

(Next page: Transfer your scores for each question.)

Spiritual Gift Assessment Scoring Sheet

- Please record your scores from the previous four pages onto this chart.
- Pay attention to the question-numbering—it counts across, not down!
- Once done, total each column to get a number for each letter.
- Then, circle your top 3-5 scores (looking at A through W).
- Note your lowest 2 scores (just looking at A through S).
- Transfer your results to the chart on page 12.

1.	2.	3.	4.	5.	6.	7.	8.	9.	10.	11.	12.
24.	25.	26.	27.	28.	29.	30.	31.	32.	33.	34.	35.
47.	48.	49.	50.	51.	52.	53.	54.	55.	56.	57.	58.
A.	B.	C.	D.	E.	F.	G.	H.	I.	J.	K.	L.

13.	14.	15.	16.	17.	18.	19.	20.	21.	22.	23.
36.	37.	38.	39.	40.	41.	42.	43.	44.	45.	46.
59.	60.	61.	62.	63.	64.	65.	66.	67.	68.	69.
M.	N.	O.	P.	Q.	R.	S.	T.	U.	V.	W.

APPENDIX B

Your Unique Design Class Form

Please complete this form and return it to your class leader.

NAME: EMAIL / PHONE:

Your Spiritual Gifts	Interests/Experience	Ministry Passions
☐ Administration	☐ Art | Media | Theatre | *Specify skills:*	☐ Administration | Organizing
☐ Apostleship		☐ Children (Early/ Elementary)
☐ Artistic Expression	☐ Mechanical | *Specify skills:*	☐ Emergent | Young Adult
☐ Craftsmanship		☐ Facilities
☐ Discernment	☐ Event Planning | *Specify skills:*	☐ Youth (Middle/ High School)
☐ Evangelism		☐ Connecting | Equipping
☐ Exhortation	☐ Baking | Cooking | Food Service | *Specify skills:*	☐ Leadership
		☐ Men's Ministry
☐ Faith		☐ Missions | Outreach
☐ Giving	☐ Helping where needed | *Specify skills:*	☐ Music | Worship
		☐ Care | Helping | Counseling
☐ Healing		☐ Senior Adults
☐ Helps	☐ Construction | Contracting | *Specify skills:*	☐ Spiritual Formation | Adult Education
☐ Hospitality		☐ University
☐ Intercession	☐ General | *Specify skills:*	☐ Welcome | Community LIfe
☐ Interpr. Tongues		☐ Women's Ministry
☐ Knowledge	☐ Music | Worship | *Specify skills:*	☐ Other Passion(s) _____ _____
☐ Leadership	☐ Technical | Office Skills | *Specify skills:*	
☐ Mercy		**NOTES**
☐ Miraculous Powers	☐ Professional Services | *Specify skills:*	
☐ Prophecy		
☐ Shepherding	☐ Teaching | Facilitating | *Specify groups / ages:*	
☐ Teaching		
☐ Tongues	☐ Other | *Specify skills:*	
☐ Wisdom		

Your Unique Design Course Evaluation

DATE(S) OF THE CLASS(ES) YOU ATTENDED : _____

PLEASE RATE THE MATERIAL PRESENTED IN THE COURSE, USING THE FOLLOWING SCALE :

1	2	3	4	5
POOR				EXCELLENT
NOT LIKELY				VERY LIKELY
NOT RELEVANT				VERY RELEVANT

1. How would you rate the value and quality of this course?

_____

2. How was your learning experience in this course?

_____

3. How relevant is what you learned to life/work/ministry?

_____

4. How likely would you be to recommend this course?

_____

5. What aspects of the course were most beneficial?

6. When we present this course again, what should we consider doing differently?

7. If we were to quote you about this class, what would you say?

8. Please comment on the written material provided.

Evaluation continued on the back

PLEASE RATE THE INSTRUCTOR(S), USING THE FOLLOWING SCALE

1	2	3	4	5
POOR				EXCELLENT

INSTRUCTOR 1 NAME: _____

INSTRUCTOR 2 NAME (if applicable):_____

9. To what extent did the instructor(s) demonstrate comfort with and understanding of the material?

INSTRUCTOR 1:

INSTRUCTOR 2:

10. To what extent did the instructor(s)' style and presentation contribute to your learning?

INSTRUCTOR 1:

INSTRUCTOR 2:

11. To what extent did the instructor(s)' interaction with class participants facilitate your learning?

INSTRUCTOR 1:

INSTRUCTOR 2:

12. Additional comments:

Please return this completed form to your class leader.

ABOUT THE AUTHOR

Shirley is passionate about helping people discover and live into their calling and purpose. Her heart's desire is to connect individuals and organizations with the resources and encouragement they need to be their best. She has guided thousands of people to understand their spiritual gifts and get involved in serving over the past three decades.

Shirley, author of the *God. Gifts. You. Your Unique Calling and Design* workbook, is a consultant, coach, facilitator who has worked with faith-based organizations, nonprofit agencies, and leaders in a diversity of organizations for over 30 years. Shirley has been EquipConnectServe Director of a 1200 member church in Boulder, Colorado since 1999.

For more information and other resources, go to: GODGIFTSYOU.COM